CASSEROLES

CASSEROLES

tasty recipes for hearty main meal stews

Katharine Blakemore

LORENZ BOOKS

NOTES

Bracketed terms are intended for American readers.

For all recipes, quantities are given in both metric and imperial measures and, where appropriate, measures are also given in standard cups and spoons. Follow one set, but not a mixture, because they are not interchangeable.

Standard spoon and cup measures are level.
1 tsp = 5ml, 1 tbsp = 15ml,
1 cup = 250ml/8fl oz

Australian standard tablespoons are 20ml. Australian readers should use 3 tsp in place of 1 tbsp for measuring small quantities of gelatine, flour, salt, etc.

Medium (US large) eggs are used unless otherwise stated.

This edition is published by Lorenz Books

Lorenz Books is an imprint of Anness Publishing Ltd
Hermes House, 88–89 Blackfriars Road, London SE1 8HA
tel. 020 7401 2077; fax 020 7633 9499
www.lorenzbooks.com; info@anness.com

© Anness Publishing Ltd 2003

This edition distributed in the UK by The Manning Partnership Ltd
6 The Old Dairy, Melcombe Road, Bath BA2 3LR
tel. 01225 478 444; fax 01225 478 440; sales@manning-partnership.co.uk

This edition distributed in the USA and Canada by National Book Network
4501 Forbes Boulevard, Suite 200, Lanham, MD 20706
tel. 301 459 3366; fax 301 429 5746; www.nbnbooks.com

This edition distributed in Australia by Pan Macmillan Australia
Level 18, St Martins Tower, 31 Market St, Sydney, NSW 2000
tel. 1300 135 113; fax 1300 135 103; customer.service@macmillan.com.au

A CIP catalogue record for this book is available from the British Library.

Publisher: Joanna Lorenz
Managing Editor: Linda Fraser
Editor: Clare Gooden
Recipes: Sarah Edmonds, Jenni Fleetwood, Brian Glover, Nicola Graimes, Lucy Knox, Lesley Mackley, Sallie Morris, Jennie Shapter, Kate Whiteman
Photography: Martin Brigdale, Janine Hosegood, William Lingwood, Thomas Odulate, Craig Robertson
Designer: Adelle Morris
Indexer: Hilary Bird

10 9 8 7 6 5 4 3 2 1

CONTENTS

Introduction

ABOVE Casseroles, such as the classic French coq au vin, are so well-loved that they are popular all over the world.

ABOVE Fresh crusty bread is all you need to accompany a casserole and is perfect for mopping up delicious leftover juices.

A casserole is the term used for a cooking method, the resulting dish and the type of pot in which it is cooked. In most cases food is slow-cooked in liquid in a covered pot either in the oven or on top of the stove. Some casseroles are much quicker to cook, however, such as those using fish, shellfish or liver.

Casseroles are easy to prepare, can be made in advance then reheated, and need little attention when cooking – an important factor in these busy times. Too often we fall back on convenience foods when, with a little forward planning, a delicious and satisfying home-cooked meal can be easily produced.

Most casseroles are one-pot meals and need to be served with only a basic accompaniment, such as mashed potatoes, rice or crusty bread.

A VERSATILE MAIN MEAL
Whether cooking for your family, for large parties or for dinner party guests, casseroles are, or should be, an important part of a cook's repertoire. For family meals, use cheaper cuts of meat and add a few well-chosen flavourings to provide an economical and nourishing meal. When cooking for large numbers a hearty one-pot dish with everything cooked in the casserole is always worth considering.

A casserole makes a memorable centrepiece to even the most elegant dinner party. Use an unusual cut of meat such as veal shin (shank) to make osso bucco, or prepare a delicate fish casserole, which can be cooked in advance and needs little attention, so the cook can relax with guests.

CASSEROLES AROUND THE WORLD
Many countries of the world have a casserole-type classic dish. Think of the curries from India and Pakistan, the wine-rich dishes from France, such as coq au vin and boeuf Bourguignonne, Irish stew and British dishes such as Lancashire hot pot. All of them are cooked in a casserole-style dish.

Often it is the name of the cooking pot that gives a dish its name. The daubes and marmites from France and the tagines from Morocco are good examples. Most casserole dishes are deep; however, the tagine differs as it is a shallow earthenware dish with a tall conical lid.

IDEAL INGREDIENTS
The long, slow and moist cooking that ingredients get while being baked in a casserole makes it a perfect method to choose when using less expensive cuts of meat, game or poultry. After being casseroled, even the toughest cut of meat will be tenderized. Cooking in a casserole is also a good way of adding extra flavour to what can sometimes be fairly bland ingredients, such as chicken.

Red meat and game should be cut into small pieces to make sure they cook evenly. Chicken is often sold cut into leg and thigh pieces. These are the best portions to use in casseroles because they do not dry out when cooked for a long time.

Fish casseroles usually cook more quickly than those made with meat and poultry – shellfish are generally added at almost the last moment to prevent them from overcooking. Any firm-fleshed fish, such as monkfish, cod or hoki, is ideal for cooking in this way. Use skinless fillets and chop them into even-sized chunks.

Root vegetables, such as carrots or sweet potatoes, and dried beans and pulses are excellent vegetarian options as they hold their shape and readily absorb other flavours.

LEFT Simple boiled rice is the ideal accompaniment for most casseroles and is relatively hassle-free to prepare, making it perfect for quick, informal family meals.

ABOVE Hearty vegetarian casseroles of dried beans and other pulses are easy, economical, delicious, satisfying and packed with nutrients.

Equipment

Casserole dishes are divided into two categories – flameproof and ovenproof – and a well-equipped cook should have at least one variety if not both.

FLAMEPROOF

The lidded flameproof casserole is probably the most useful dish available. It can be used on the stove for browning and sizzling ingredients at the start of a recipe, and can then be transferred straight to the oven to finish cooking.

Flameproof casseroles are often made of metal, the most popular being the enamel-lined cast-iron pots, but they can also be made of toughened glass. They come in a variety of sizes, colours and designs, and retain the heat very well, meaning they are ideal for serving casseroles straight to the table.

OVENPROOF

Shallow ovenproof dishes are perfect for casseroles that do not need to be covered when cooking. Recipes that have a topping, like sliced potatoes or the delicious savoury breadcrumb layer used to top a cassoulet, should be left uncovered in the oven so that the topping browns nicely and becomes crisp.

Deep ovenproof casseroles can be made of earthenware, china, toughened glass or pottery. They are often sold without lids so, depending on the recipe, you may need to cover them with foil during cooking to prevent the casserole from burning.

The right dish can make all the difference and a combination of flameproof and ovenproof casseroles in different shapes and sizes would be very useful in most kitchens.

DUTCH OVENS

If storage space limits you to just one piece of casserole equipment, then a large, heavy, two-handled pan with a tight-fitting lid, known as a Dutch oven, is probably the best option.

Thought to have been invented by German settlers in the US state of Pennsylvania in the 16th century, the name Dutch oven is a corruption of Deutsch, meaning German. Dutch ovens are extremely versatile – they can be used on the stove, in the oven, on a barbecue or even over a campfire.

A Dutch oven is most commonly used to prepare traditional pot roasts, where a whole joint of meat or a whole bird is braised in liquid. However, it can also be used for most other casserole recipes and is ideal if you are cooking for a crowd or making large quantities of a casserole to freeze.

ABOVE Flameproof casseroles can be used either on the stove or in the oven.

ABOVE Most casseroles can be transferred from the oven to the table for serving.

ABOVE A Dutch oven is one of the most useful pieces of equipment in a kitchen.

Making Casseroles

Casseroling is a moist, slow method of cooking in the oven or on the stove.

SIMPLE MEAT CASSEROLE

The meat is simmered at a low temperature in liquid – wine, water, beer or stock. This is ideal for tough, inexpensive cuts, such as shin, leg, brisket, thin flank or chuck and blade, as the cooking time allows the meat to tenderize. Stewing steak is tougher and needs longer cooking than braising steak. Tough cuts should be cut into large pieces because they are cooked for a longer time. More tender meats can be cut into smaller chunks.

1 Preheat the oven to 180°C/350°F/Gas 4. Trim off any fat and cut the meat into 2.5cm/1in cubes.

2 Toss the cubes of meat in seasoned plain (all-purpose) flour, shaking off any excess. The flour will brown when cooking to give the casserole extra flavour and thicken the sauce.

3 Heat some oil in a large flameproof casserole, add the meat in batches and cook until evenly browned. Remove the meat from the casserole and set aside.

4 Add a selection of vegetables to the casserole and braise in the oil and meat juices for about 5 minutes.

5 Return the meat to the casserole, then add some herbs or spices and the cooking liquid. Season to taste. Bring to the boil, cover and cook in the oven for 1½–2 hours, or until the meat is tender.

6 Remove the casserole from the oven. If it needs to be thickened, use one of the methods listed below. Alternatively, the casserole can be put back onto the stove and the liquid boiled rapidly until it has reduced by about half its volume.

How to thicken a casserole

If a casserole has not been thickened during the initial stages of cooking, for example by the meat being coated in plain (all-purpose) flour before browning, then the liquid can be thickened towards the end of cooking time using cornflour (cornstarch).

Cornflour can be mixed with a little cold water or cool cooking liquid to make a smooth paste, then stirred slowly into the casserole. It will need to be simmered for a short time to allow the starch to cook and the mixture to thicken.

Another option is to mix together equal quantities of butter and plain flour to make a paste – this is known as beurre manié. Whisk small amounts at a time into the cooking liquid to thicken the sauce.

Alternatively, rice or a grain such as barley can be added to the casserole part-way through cooking. Fresh breadcrumbs stirred in towards the end of the cooking time will also thicken the liquid.

CASEROLING POULTRY AND WHOLE GAME BIRDS

Whole birds as well as pieces can be casseroled. If using poultry pieces, choose thighs or legs as these won't dry out when cooked for a long time. When casseroling whole birds the shape and size of the dish you use is very important. It should be big enough to hold the bird, the cooking liquid and any vegetables you might add, yet still allow enough room for the bird to be turned if necessary. Use an oval flameproof casserole with a tight-fitting lid if you have one – this is the best option because it means that the poultry can be browned on the stove first before being put into the oven. The herbs or spices will add flavour, and the cooking liquid will moisten the meat.

1 Heat some oil in a large, flameproof casserole. Add the poultry pieces and cook, turning them until they are golden brown all over.

2 Alternatively, if using a whole bird, brown the bird all over. Remove the bird or poultry pieces from the casserole before adding the vegetables to the fat remaining in the pan. Cook gently to soften the vegetables.

3 Replace the poultry before adding the chosen liquid – stock, wine or canned tomatoes. Season well, then bring just to simmering point. Cover with a tight lid and simmer very gently on top of the stove, or cook in the oven at 180°C/350°F/Gas 4 until the meat and vegetables are cooked through.

CASEROLING FISH AND SHELLFISH

Fish and shellfish should be added towards the end of the cooking time as they can quickly become overcooked. If making a fish casserole in advance, add the fish when reheating.

1 Heat the oil then fry the vegetables until golden brown. Add the chopped tomatoes and fish stock, bring to the boil and simmer for about 20 minutes.

2 Stir in the fish chunks, cover and simmer for about 15–20 minutes until the fish is cooked through.

Making Fresh Stock

A well-flavoured stock is the basis of a good casserole. Although there are many packets and cubes available, nothing beats the home-made version. Meat stock is made with bones and vegetables, while vegetable stock relies on the flavours of root vegetables and herbs. It is well worth making large batches of stock and freezing them for later use.

Flavourings should never overpower a dish but should subtly enhance and complement the main ingredients. Avoid adding any vegetables that are particularly strong-tasting. Initially, be sparing with basic seasonings such as salt and pepper. When the liquid is reduced, these flavours can intensify and ruin a dish. It is much better to check the seasoning before serving and add more if necessary.

MEAT STOCK
This makes a light-coloured stock. If a darker stock is required, then the bones and vegetables can be roasted in the oven for 30 minutes before adding to the pan with the vegetables.

675g/1½lb beef or veal bones

1 onion, sliced

1 celery stick, sliced

1 carrot, sliced

bouquet garni or 1 fresh thyme sprig and 6 parsley stalks

1.5 litres/2½ pints/6¼ cups water

salt and ground black pepper

1 If the butcher has not already chopped the bones for you, chop them into pieces small enough to fit into your largest pan.

2 Put the bones, vegetables, herbs and seasoning into the pan. Pour in the water, bring to the boil, then use a slotted spoon to remove any scum that might have formed on top.

3 Partially cover the pan, reduce the heat to low and simmer gently for 2–3 hours. Strain the stock into a bowl, then leave to cool.

4 If possible, chill the stock overnight so that any fat that solidifies and accumulates on top can easily be removed with a slotted spoon.

Successful stock making

A stock is only ever as good as its ingredients. Use fresh vegetables and peel or wash well first. Trim off any visible fat from bones before you start. Skim off as much scum as you can when bringing the mixture to the boil. To make a really clear stock, add 250ml/8fl oz/1 cup cold water or crushed ice and skim off the scum again. Do not stir the stock while it is simmering if you want to keep it clear. Take care not to add too much salt, as it can become concentrated during cooking.

ABOVE Meat stock adds a rich flavour to many dishes – trim any fat off the bones before adding them to the pan.

ABOVE Vegetable stock is a good choice for delicate dishes, such as fish stew, as well as vegetarian casseroles.

Adding Flavour to Casseroles

There are various simple ways of adding extra flavour to casseroles. Onions, garlic and almost any other vegetables can be added for endless combinations of flavours; fresh herbs, either in a bouquet garni or tucked among the ingredients, give casseroles a delicious aroma and distinctive taste; whole or ground spices are often used to liven things up; and a splash of red or white wine, depending on the recipe, adds a rich flavour and gives even the simplest casseroles an extra kick. However, it is often necessary to add ingredients at different times to get the maximum flavour.

ABOVE Mushrooms can be added at the beginning of cooking to allow their flavour to permeate the casserole.

VEGETABLES

Almost any vegetable can be casseroled but they should not all be added at the same time. Aromatic ingredients, such as onions and garlic, should be added at the beginning so that they add maximum flavour. Root vegetables, such as carrots, swede (rutabaga), turnips and potatoes are usually added early on because they take a long time to cook. More tender vegetables, such as green beans, peas, asparagus and courgettes (zucchini), should not be overcooked. They taste better when still slightly crisp, so make sure that you add these towards the end of the cooking time. Mushrooms, although they cook fairly quickly, are usually added early on to allow time for their flavour to intensify.

ABOVE When using garlic, remember that the flavour intensifies significantly if a casserole is frozen and then reheated.

> ### Adding liquids to casseroles
> In most recipes the liquid – water, stock, wine, beer, (hard) cider or even fruit juice – is added at the start of cooking. This should always be boiling when the casserole is put into the oven. Some of the liquid will often evaporate during the cooking process. This can happen if the casserole is not well sealed with a lid or foil. If more liquid needs to be added to the casserole, then it should be hot too. This not only avoids a sudden temperature change, but also makes sure that the ingredients are not cooled too much, which would result in a prolonged cooking time.

WINE

Using red or white wine in a casserole has two main advantages. It adds a delicious rich flavour and the acidity of the wine also helps to break down the fibres of the meat, making tougher cuts more tender and succulent. If time permits, the meat can be marinated in wine before cooking to give extra flavour and tenderness. Using red wine also adds a deep, rich colour to casseroles.

The quality of the wine used in a casserole will affect the overall taste. For special occasions, it is worth buying a fairly good bottle – it will make all the difference.

HERBS

Use fresh herbs whenever possible. Stirring chopped fresh herbs into a finished casserole can add a delicate aroma and a wealth of flavour as well as colour, while sprinkling them over a finished dish just before serving makes a pretty garnish. Add them at the last minute because they lose their potency when cooked.

Making a bouquet garni

A bundle of fresh herbs tied together with kitchen string or a strip of celery or leek can be added to casseroles for extra flavour. The classic combination is 1–2 bay leaves, 2–3 parsley sprigs and 1 thyme sprig. In Provence rosemary is always included and in Italy sage and rosemary are often added. In some dishes, a strip of orange rind is also included. Discard the bouquet garni before serving.

If fresh herbs are not available use dried herbs. These have a more concentrated flavour than fresh ones so they should be used sparingly. Always make sure you allow sufficient time for them to rehydrate and soften.

Some herbs are traditionally paired with certain meats because they are known to complement each other particularly well. Classic combinations include: sage with pork; thyme with beef; rosemary or mint with lamb; tarragon with chicken; dill with fish; parsley or chives with vegetables and bay leaves with pot roasts.

SPICES

When using spices they can either be ground and added to the seasoned flour that coats the meat or added, whole or ground, to the pan along with the vegetables. Add them at the beginning of cooking whenever possible, as some spices need to be cooked to impart their flavour.

Chilli, whether hot or mild, fresh or dried, is an essential ingredient of many cuisines, including Indian, Thai and Mexican. Moroccan and other North African recipes tend to use sweeter-flavoured, warm spices, such as ginger, cinnamon and cumin.

The flavours of spices intensify on reheating, particularly if a casserole has been frozen, so if you are planning to cook in advance you may want to reduce the quantities slightly.

ABOVE When using ground spices to flavour casseroles, fry them gently to release their flavour before adding liquid.

ABOVE Fresh root ginger can be grated or finely chopped. It adds an exotic note to the flavour of a simple casserole.

MEAT and GAME

This chapter is full of ideas that will transform a simple meat casserole into something a little different. For special occasions, impress your guests with Spicy Venison Casserole or delicate Italian Osso Bucco with Risotto Milanese. For a family dinner, try something more traditional such as simple Lamb's Liver and Bacon Casserole or classic Boeuf Bourguignonne.

Boeuf Bourguignonne

The classic French dish of beef cooked Burgundy-style, with red wine, bacon, shallots and mushrooms, is simmered gently at a low temperature. Using top rump or braising steak reduces the cooking time.

INGREDIENTS | SERVES SIX

175g/6oz rindless streaky (fatty) bacon rashers (strips), chopped

900g/2lb lean braising steak, such as top rump (round) of beef

30ml/2 tbsp plain (all-purpose) flour

45ml/3 tbsp sunflower oil

25g/1oz/2 tbsp butter

12 shallots, peeled but left whole

2 garlic cloves, crushed

175g/6oz/2¹⁄₃ cups sliced mushrooms

450ml/³⁄₄ pint/scant 2 cups robust red wine

150ml/¹⁄₄ pint/²⁄₃ cup beef stock

1 bay leaf

2 sprigs each of fresh thyme, parsley and marjoram

salt and ground black pepper

1 Preheat the oven to 160°C/325°F/Gas 3. Heat a large flameproof casserole on the hob (stovetop), then add the bacon and cook, stirring occasionally, until the pieces are crisp and golden brown.

2 Meanwhile, cut the meat into 2.5cm/1in cubes. Season the flour and use to coat the meat. Use a slotted spoon to remove the bacon from the casserole and set aside. Add and heat the oil, then brown the beef, in batches, and set aside with the bacon.

3 Add the butter to the fat remaining in the casserole. Add the shallots and garlic and cook, stirring, for about 5 minutes, until just starting to colour, then add the mushrooms and cook for a further 5 minutes.

4 Return the bacon and meat to the casserole, and stir in the wine and stock. Tie the bay leaf, thyme, parsley and marjoram together into a bouquet garni with kitchen string and add to the casserole.

5 Cover and cook in the oven for 1½ hours, or until the meat is tender, stirring once or twice. Season to taste, discard the bouquet garni and serve the casserole with creamy mashed root vegetables.

COOK'S TIP

• Boeuf Bourguignonne freezes very well. Transfer the mixture to a cold dish so that it cools quickly, then pour it into a rigid plastic container. Push the cubes of meat down into the sauce or they will dry out. Freeze for up to 2 months. Thaw overnight in the refrigerator, then transfer to a flameproof casserole and add 150ml/¹⁄₄ pint/²⁄₃ cup water. Stir well and bring to the boil, stirring occasionally, then cover and simmer for at least 10 minutes, or until the meat is piping hot.

VARIATION

• Use lardons, which are available from large supermarkets, instead of bacon for an even more authentic result.

Osso Bucco with Risotto Milanese

The name of this dish means "bone with a hole". It is a traditional Milanese casserole of veal, onions and leeks in white wine for which golden-coloured risotto Milanese is the classic accompaniment.

1 Heat the butter and oil in a large frying pan until sizzling. Add the onion and leek, and cook gently, stirring occasionally, for about 5 minutes without browning the onions. Season the flour and toss the veal in it, then add the meat to the pan and cook over a high heat until it is brown.

2 Gradually stir in the wine and heat until simmering. Cover the pan and simmer for 1½ hours, stirring occasionally, or until the meat is very tender. Use a slotted spoon to transfer the veal to a warm dish, then boil the sauce quickly until reduced and thickened to the required consistency.

3 Make the risotto about 30 minutes before the end of the cooking time. Melt the butter in a large pan. Add the onion and cook, stirring occasionally, until soft.

4 Stir in the rice, coating all the grains in butter. Add a ladleful of boiling chicken stock and mix well.

5 Continue adding the boiling stock, a ladleful at a time, allowing each portion to be absorbed before adding the next. The whole process should take about 20 minutes. Add the veal to the pan.

6 Pound the saffron threads in a mortar, then stir in the wine. Add the saffron-flavoured wine to the risotto and cook for a final 5 minutes. Remove the pan from the heat and stir in the Parmesan.

7 Mix the lemon rind, parsley and garlic for the gremolata. Spoon some risotto on to each plate, then add some veal. Sprinkle with gremolata and serve immediately.

COOK'S TIPS

• Buy veal shin (shank) thickly cut so the pieces retain the marrow during cooking.
• A mezzaluna (double-handled, half-moon shaped chopping blade) is ideal for preparing gremolata ingredients. If using a food processor, avoid over-processing.

INGREDIENTS | SERVES FOUR

50g/2oz/¼ cup butter

15ml/1 tbsp olive oil

1 large onion, chopped

1 leek, finely chopped

45ml/3 tbsp plain (all-purpose) flour

4 large portions of veal shin (shank), hind cut

600ml/1 pint/2½ cups dry white wine

salt and ground black pepper

FOR THE RISOTTO

25g/1oz/2 tbsp butter

1 onion, finely chopped

350g/12oz/1²/₃ cups risotto rice

1 litre/1¾ pints/4 cups boiling chicken stock

2.5ml/½ tsp saffron threads

60ml/4 tbsp white wine

50g/2oz/²/₃ cup coarsely grated Parmesan cheese

FOR THE GREMOLATA

grated rind of 1 lemon

30ml/2 tbsp chopped fresh parsley

1 garlic clove, finely chopped

Lamb's Liver and Bacon Casserole

Lamb's liver is flavourful and very tender, providing that it is not overcooked. Boiled new potatoes tossed in lots of butter and green beans go well with this simple, quick, yet deliciously comforting casserole.

INGREDIENTS | **SERVES FOUR**

30ml/2 tbsp sunflower oil

225g/8oz rindless unsmoked back (lean) bacon rashers (strips), cut into pieces

2 onions, halved and sliced

175g/6oz/2⅓ cups chestnut mushrooms, halved

450g/1lb lamb's liver, trimmed and sliced

25g/1oz/2 tbsp butter

15ml/1 tbsp soy sauce

30ml/2 tbsp plain (all-purpose) flour

150ml/¼ pint/⅔ cup chicken stock

salt and ground black pepper

1 Heat the oil in a large frying pan or shallow, flameproof casserole, add the bacon and cook over a medium heat, stirring frequently, until crisp.

2 Add the onion slices to the pan and cook over a low heat for about 10 minutes, until softened but not browned. Add the mushrooms and cook for 1 minute more.

3 Use a slotted spoon to remove the bacon and vegetables from the pan and set them aside. Increase the heat to high, add the liver to the pan and cook, turning once, for 3–4 minutes to seal the slices on both sides. Remove the liver from the pan, set aside and keep warm.

4 Melt the butter in the pan, add the soy sauce and sprinkle in the flour, then blend thoroughly together with a wooden spoon. Gradually stir in the chicken stock and bring to the boil, stirring constantly until the sauce is thickened and smooth.

5 Return the liver and vegetables to the pan and heat through for 1 minute. Season with salt and pepper to taste and serve immediately with new potatoes and lightly cooked green beans.

COOK'S TIPS

• To prepare liver, snip and peel off the fine membrane covering it, if this has not already been done. Cut the liver diagonally into even slices. Using kitchen scissors, snip out any tough internal tubes.

• For best results, make sure that the liver is thinly sliced.

• The trick when cooking liver is to seal it quickly, then simmer it gently and briefly. Prolonged or fierce cooking makes liver hard and grainy.

VARIATION

• For a special treat, use calf's liver which is extremely tender and delicately flavoured. Even children, not usually great fans of liver, will probably like this.

Cassoulet de Languedoc

There are many variations of this classic French casserole of sausage, beans and assorted meats. In Languedoc alone, Toulouse, Castelnaudary and Carcassonne all claim to be the historical home of cassoulet.

1 Drain and rinse the beans well, then place them in a large, heavy pan and add the onion chunks, carrot quarters, cloves and parsley stalks. Pour in just enough cold water to cover the beans completely and bring to the boil.

2 Boil the beans vigorously for 10 minutes, then reduce the heat, cover and simmer for about 1½ hours, or until the beans are tender. Skim off any scum with a spoon and top up the pan with boiling water as necessary. Drain the cooked beans, reserving the cooking liquid. Discard the onion, carrot, cloves and parsley stalks.

3 Put the gammon into another pan and pour in enough cold water to cover. Bring to the boil, reduce the heat to low and then simmer for 10 minutes. Drain and discard the water and set the gammon aside until cool enough to handle, then cut the meat into bitesize chunks. Preheat the oven to 150°C/300°F/Gas 2.

4 Heat a large flameproof casserole and cook the duck quarters, in batches, until golden on all sides. Remove the duck from the casserole and set aside. Add and brown the cubed lamb in batches.

5 Pour off fat from the casserole to leave about 30ml/2 tbsp. Add the chopped onion and garlic and cook gently until softened. Stir in the wine and remove from the heat.

6 Spoon a layer of beans into the casserole. Add the duck, then the lamb, gammon, sausage, tomatoes and more beans. Season each layer as you add the ingredients. Pour in enough of the reserved cooking liquid to cover the ingredients. Cover and cook in the oven for 2½ hours. Check occasionally to make sure that the beans are covered with liquid and add more stock if necessary.

7 Mix together the topping ingredients and then sprinkle over the cassoulet. Cook, uncovered, for a further 30 minutes.

INGREDIENTS | **SERVES EIGHT**

225g/8oz/1¼ cups dried haricot (navy) beans, soaked in cold water for 24 hours

2 large onions, 1 cut into chunks and 1 chopped

1 large carrot, quartered

2 cloves

small handful of fresh parsley stalks

225g/8oz lean gammon (smoked or cured ham), in one piece

4 duck leg quarters, split into thighs and drumsticks

225g/8oz lean, boneless lamb, trimmed and cubed

2 garlic cloves, finely chopped

75ml/5 tbsp dry white wine

175g/6oz cooked Toulouse sausage, or garlic sausage, skinned and coarsely chopped

400g/14oz can chopped tomatoes

salt and ground black pepper

FOR THE TOPPING

75g/3oz/1½ cups fresh white breadcrumbs

30ml/2 tbsp chopped fresh parsley

2 garlic cloves, finely chopped

Lamb Stew with Shallots and New Potatoes

INGREDIENTS | **SERVES SIX**

1kg/2¼lb boneless shoulder of lamb, trimmed of fat and cut into 5cm/2in cubes

1 garlic clove, finely chopped

finely grated rind of ½ lemon and juice of 1 lemon

90ml/6 tbsp olive oil

45ml/3 tbsp plain (all-purpose) flour

1 large onion, sliced

5 anchovy fillets in olive oil, drained

2.5ml/½ tsp caster (superfine) sugar

300ml/½ pint/1¼ cups fruity white wine

475ml/16fl oz/2 cups lamb stock or half stock and half water

1 fresh bay leaf

1 fresh thyme sprig

1 fresh parsley sprig

500g/1¼lb small new potatoes

250g/9oz shallots, peeled but left whole

45ml/3 tbsp double (heavy) cream (optional)

salt and ground black pepper

FOR THE TOPPING

shredded rind of ½ lemon

45ml/3 tbsp chopped fresh flat leaf parsley

1 garlic clove, chopped

This fresh, lemon-seasoned lamb casserole is finished with the traditional Italian topping of chopped garlic, parsley and lemon rind, which gives it a distinctive flavour.

1 Mix the lamb, garlic, rind and half the lemon juice. Season, then add 15ml/1 tbsp olive oil and marinate for 12–24 hours.

2 Drain the lamb, reserving the marinade, and pat the meat dry with kitchen paper. Preheat the oven to 180°C/350°F/Gas 4.

3 Heat 30ml/2 tbsp olive oil in a large, heavy frying pan. Season the flour and toss the meat in it, shaking off any excess. Fry the lamb, in batches, and transfer to a flameproof casserole when browned. Add an extra 15ml/1 tbsp olive oil if needed.

4 Reduce the heat, add another 15ml/1 tbsp oil to the pan and cook the onion gently for 10 minutes, stirring frequently. Add the anchovies and sugar, mashing the fish well.

5 Add the reserved marinade, increase the heat and cook for 2 minutes. Add the wine and stock, and bring to the boil. Simmer for 5 minutes. Pour over the lamb.

6 Tie the bay leaf, thyme and parsley together into a bouquet garni with kitchen string and add to the casserole. Season to taste with salt and pepper, then cover tightly and cook in the oven for 1 hour. Add the potatoes, re-cover the casserole and cook for a further 20 minutes.

7 Meanwhile, chop all the topping ingredients together finely. Set aside.

8 Heat the remaining oil in a frying pan and brown the shallots, then add them to the lamb. Cover and cook for 30–40 minutes, until the lamb is tender. Transfer the lamb and vegetables to a serving dish to keep warm. Discard the herbs.

9 Transfer the casserole to the hob (stovetop) and boil the cooking juices to reduce them. Add the cream, if using, and simmer for 2–3 minutes. Season and add lemon juice to taste. Pour the sauce over the lamb, sprinkle over the topping and serve.

Pork Casserole with Onions, Chilli and Dried Fruit

Inspired by South American cooking, a *mole* – paste – of chilli, shallots and nuts is added to this casserole of pork and onions. Part of the *mole* is added at the end of cooking to retain its fresh flavour.

INGREDIENTS | **SERVES SIX**

25ml/1¹/₂ tbsp plain (all-purpose) flour

1kg/2¹/₄lb shoulder or leg of pork, cut into 5cm/2in cubes

45–60ml/3–4 tbsp olive oil

2 large onions, chopped

2 garlic cloves, finely chopped

600ml/1 pint/2¹/₂ cups fruity white wine

105ml/7 tbsp water

115g/4oz/¹/₂ cup ready-to-eat dried apricots

115g/4oz/¹/₂ cup ready-to-eat prunes

grated rind and juice of 1 small orange

pinch of muscovado (brown) sugar (optional)

30ml/2 tbsp chopped fresh parsley

¹/₂–1 fresh green chilli, seeded and finely chopped (optional)

salt and ground black pepper

FOR THE MOLE

3 ancho and 2 pasilla chillies (or 5 large dried red chillies)

30ml/2 tbsp olive oil

2 shallots, chopped

2 garlic cloves, chopped

1 fresh green chilli, seeded and chopped

10ml/2 tsp ground coriander

5ml/1 tsp mild Spanish paprika

50g/2oz/¹/₂ cup blanched almonds, toasted

15ml/1 tbsp chopped fresh oregano or 2.5ml/¹/₂ tsp dried

1 To make the mole paste, toast the dried chillies in a dry frying pan over a low heat for 1–2 minutes, until aromatic, then soak them in warm water for 30 minutes.

2 Drain the chillies, reserving the soaking water, and discard their stalks and seeds. Preheat the oven to 160°C/325°F/Gas 3.

3 Heat the oil in a small frying pan. Cook the shallots, garlic, fresh green chilli and coriander over a low heat for 5 minutes.

4 Transfer the shallot mixture to a food processor or blender and add the drained chillies, paprika, almonds and oregano. Blend, adding 45–60ml/3–4 tbsp of the chilli soaking liquid to make a paste.

5 Season the flour with salt and pepper, then toss the pork in it. Heat 45ml/3 tbsp of the oil in a large frying pan and fry the pork, stirring frequently, until sealed. Transfer to a flameproof casserole.

6 If necessary, add the remaining olive oil to the frying pan and heat. Add the onions and garlic and cook over a low heat, stirring occasionally for 8–10 minutes.

7 Add the wine and measured water to the frying pan and cook for 2 minutes. Stir in half the mole paste and bubble for a few seconds before pouring the mixture over the pork.

8 Season lightly, stir well, then cover and cook in the oven for 1¹/₂ hours.

9 Increase the oven temperature to 180°C/350°F/Gas 4. Add the apricots, prunes, orange juice and sugar, if using. Cover and cook for 30–45 minutes.

10 Transfer the casserole to the hob (stovetop) and stir in the remaining mole. Simmer for 5 minutes. Serve sprinkled with the orange rind, parsley and fresh chilli, if using.

Spicy Venison Casserole

Being low in fat but high in flavour, venison makes excellent healthy, yet rich casseroles. Cranberries and orange bring a festive fruitiness to this spicy recipe. Serve with small baked potatoes and green vegetables.

INGREDIENTS | SERVES FOUR

30ml/2 tbsp olive oil

1 onion, chopped

2 celery sticks, sliced

10ml/2 tsp ground allspice

15ml/1 tbsp plain
(all-purpose) flour

675g/1^{1}/$_{2}$lb stewing
venison, cubed

225g/8oz/2 cups fresh or
frozen cranberries

grated rind and juice of
1 orange

900ml/1^{1}/$_{2}$ pints/3^{3}/$_{4}$ cups beef
or venison stock

salt and ground black pepper

1 Heat the oil in a flameproof casserole. Add the onion and celery and cook over a low heat, stirring occasionally, for about 5 minutes, or until softened.

2 Meanwhile, mix the ground allspice with the flour and either spread the mixture out on a large plate or place it in a large plastic bag. Toss a few pieces of venison at a time (to prevent them from becoming soggy) in the flour mixture until they are all lightly coated. Shake off any excess.

3 When the onion and celery are softened, remove from the casserole using a slotted spoon and set aside. Add the venison pieces to the casserole, in batches, and cook, stirring occasionally, until browned and sealed on all sides. Remove from the pan and set aside.

4 Add the cranberries, orange rind and juice to the casserole, together with the beef or venison stock, and stir well.

5 Return the vegetables and all the venison to the casserole and heat until simmering, then cover tightly and reduce the heat to low. Simmer gently, stirring occasionally, for about 45 minutes, or until the venison and vegetables are tender.

6 Taste the venison casserole and season with salt and pepper as required before serving with baked potatoes and a green vegetable, such as broccoli.

VARIATIONS

• Farmed venison is increasingly easy to find and is available from good butchers and many large supermarkets. It makes a rich and flavourful casserole, but lean pork or braising steak could be used in place of the venison, if you prefer.
• You could also replace the cranberries with pitted and halved ready-to-eat prunes or with redcurrants.
• For extra flavour, use either ale or stout instead of about half of the stock.

POULTRY and GAME BIRDS

Chicken is the mainstay of many family meals and with clever use of herbs, spices and wine, it can be turned into wonderfully flavourful dishes. If you have not tried them before, now is the time to experiment with guinea fowl and pigeon with these simple, yet delicious recipes.

Coq au Vin

This French country casserole was traditionally made with an old boiling fowl, marinated overnight in red wine to begin the process of tenderization, then simmered gently until completely tender.

1 Heat the oil in a large, flameproof casserole, add the shallots and cook for 5 minutes, or until golden.

2 Increase the heat, add the bacon, garlic and mushrooms and cook, stirring frequently, for a further 10 minutes. Use a slotted spoon to transfer the cooked ingredients to a plate.

3 Add the chicken portions to the casserole and cook in the oil remaining in the pan, turning them frequently until they are golden brown all over. Return the shallots, garlic, mushrooms and bacon to the casserole and pour in the red wine.

4 Tie all the ingredients for the bouquet garni in a bundle in a small piece of muslin (cheesecloth) and add it to the casserole. Bring to the boil, then lower the heat and cover the casserole. Simmer gently for about 30–40 minutes, until the chicken is tender and cooked through.

5 To make the beurre manié, cream the butter and flour together in a small bowl using your fingers or the back of a spoon to make a smooth paste.

6 Add small lumps of this paste to the bubbling casserole, stirring well until each piece has melted into the liquid before adding the next. When all the paste has been fully incorporated, bring back to the boil and simmer for 5 minutes.

7 Season the casserole to taste with salt and pepper and serve garnished with chopped fresh parsley and accompanied by boiled potatoes.

COOK'S TIPS

• Modern recipes use tender roasting birds to save time, and because boiling fowl are not readily available.
• Morels are the traditional mushrooms for this recipe so, if they are available, do·buy them as they have an affinity with chicken.

INGREDIENTS | SERVES SIX

45ml/3 tbsp light olive oil

12 shallots, peeled but left whole

225g/8oz rindless streaky (fatty) bacon rashers (strips), chopped

3 garlic cloves, finely chopped

225g/8oz/3 cups small mushrooms, halved

6 boneless chicken thigh portions

3 boneless chicken breast portions, halved

1 bottle (750ml/1¼ pints/ 3 cups) red wine

salt and ground black pepper

45ml/3 tbsp chopped fresh parsley, to garnish

FOR THE BOUQUET GARNI

3 sprigs each of fresh parsley, thyme and sage

1 bay leaf

4 peppercorns

FOR THE BEURRE MANIÉ

25g/1oz/2 tbsp butter, softened

25g/1oz/¼ cup plain (all-purpose) flour

Chicken Casserole with Winter Vegetables

INGREDIENTS | SERVES FOUR

350g/12oz onions

350g/12oz leeks

225g/8oz carrots

450g/1lb swede (rutabaga)

30ml/2 tbsp vegetable oil

4 chicken portions, about
900g/2lb total weight

115g/4oz/$\frac{1}{2}$ cup green lentils

475ml/16fl oz/2 cups
chicken stock

300ml/$\frac{1}{2}$ pint/1$\frac{1}{4}$ cups
apple juice

10ml/2 tsp cornflour
(cornstarch)

45ml/3 tbsp crème fraîche

10ml/2 tsp wholegrain mustard

30ml/2 tbsp chopped
fresh tarragon

salt and ground black pepper

fresh tarragon sprigs,
to garnish

A deliciously creamy casserole of wonderfully tender chicken, root vegetables and lentils. Finished with crème fraîche, mustard and tarragon, this is guaranteed to keep out the cold.

1 Preheat the oven to 190°C/375°F/Gas 5. Prepare the onions, leeks, carrots and swede by coarsely chopping them.

2 Heat the oil in a large, flameproof casserole. Season the chicken portions with plenty of salt and pepper and brown them in the hot oil until golden. Remove from the casserole and drain on kitchen paper.

3 Add the onions to the casserole and cook over a low heat, stirring occasionally, for about 5 minutes, until they begin to soften and colour. Increase the heat to medium, add the leeks, carrots, swede and lentils to the casserole and cook, stirring constantly, for 2 minutes.

4 Return the chicken portions to the casserole, then add the stock, apple juice and season to taste with salt and pepper. Bring to the boil and cover tightly. Cook in the oven for 50–60 minutes, or until the chicken and lentils are tender.

5 Place the casserole on the hob (stovetop) over a medium heat. In a small bowl, blend the cornflour with about 30ml/2 tbsp water to make a smooth paste. Add the mixture to the casserole, then stir in the crème fraîche, mustard and chopped tarragon. Taste and adjust the seasoning if necessary, then simmer gently, stirring constantly, for about 2 minutes, until slightly thickened, before serving, garnished with tarragon sprigs.

COOK'S TIPS
• Chop the vegetables into even-sized pieces so that they all cook evenly.
• Green lentils are more suitable for this casserole than the smaller yellow or red varieties, as they keep their shape well and are less inclined to break down during cooking. The tiny grey-green lentils from Puy in France, which many people consider have the best flavour, would be good too, as they also retain their colour and texture. They are sometimes quite difficult to find, but are worth looking for.

Chicken Gumbo with Okra and Ham

This colourful, traditional Creole dish is really more like a very hearty soup than a casserole, but it is usually served on a bed of rice to make a delicious and substantial main course.

INGREDIENTS | **SERVES FOUR**

30ml/2 tbsp olive oil

1 onion, chopped

225g/8oz skinless, boneless chicken breast portions, cut into small chunks

25g/1oz/¹/₄ cup plain (all-purpose) flour

5ml/1 tsp paprika

30ml/2 tbsp tomato purée (paste)

600ml/1 pint/2¹/₂ cups chicken stock

400g/14oz can chopped tomatoes with herbs

a few drops of Tabasco sauce

175g/6oz okra, cut in half if large

1 red, orange or yellow (bell) pepper, seeded and chopped

2 celery sticks, sliced

225g/8oz/1¹/₃ cups diced lean cooked ham

225g/8oz large prawns (shrimp), peeled, deveined and heads removed, but with tails intact

salt and ground black pepper

boiled rice, to serve

1 Preheat the oven to 180°C/350°F/Gas 4.

2 Heat the oil in a large frying pan, add the chopped onion and cook over a medium heat, stirring occasionally, for about 5 minutes, until softened and lightly golden.

3 Add the chicken chunks to the pan and cook for 1–2 minutes, to seal. Stir in the flour, paprika and tomato purée and cook, stirring constantly, for 1–2 minutes.

4 Gradually stir in the chicken stock, then bring the sauce to the boil, stirring constantly. Add the chopped tomatoes with the juice from the can, then remove the pan from the heat. Add a few drops of Tabasco sauce and season to taste with salt and pepper.

5 Place the okra in a casserole with the red, orange or yellow pepper and the celery. Add the chicken and tomato mixture and stir well to mix.

6 Cover the casserole, transfer to the oven and cook for 30 minutes.

7 Remove the casserole from the oven, then add the ham and prawns and stir well. Cover the casserole and return it to the oven for about 10 minutes, or until the ham is heated through and the prawns are just cooked. To serve, ladle the gumbo over hot boiled rice.

COOK'S TIP
• When buying okra look for firm, bright green pods that are less than 10cm/4in long. Avoid any that are starting to turn brown at the tips.

VARIATIONS
• Replace the ham with crab or cooked, shelled mussels. For a special occasion, replace the prawns with crayfish and the ham with cooked, shelled oysters.
• Use 2.5ml/¹/₂ tsp chilli powder instead of Tabasco sauce.

Guinea Fowl and Spring Vegetable Stew

Mild, sweet leeks are excellent in this light casserole of guinea fowl and spring vegetables. More strongly flavoured than chicken with a slight hint of game, guinea fowl is deliciously tender.

1 Heat 30ml/2 tbsp of the oil in a large frying pan and cook the pancetta over a medium heat until lightly browned, stirring occasionally. Remove and set aside.

2 Season the flour with salt and pepper and toss the guinea fowl portions in it. Cook in the oil remaining in the pan until browned. Transfer to a flameproof casserole. Preheat the oven to 180°C/350°F/Gas 4.

3 Add the remaining oil to the pan and cook the onion gently until soft. Add the garlic and cook for 3–4 minutes, then stir in the pancetta and wine.

4 Tie the herbs together, add to the pan and bring to the boil. Simmer for 3–4 minutes. Pour over the guinea fowl and season. Cover and cook in the oven for 40 minutes.

5 Add the baby carrots and turnips to the casserole and cook for a further 30 minutes, or until the vegetables are just tender.

6 Stir in the leeks and cook for a further 15–20 minutes, or until all the vegetables are fully cooked.

7 Meanwhile, blanch the peas in boiling water for 2 minutes, then drain. Transfer the guinea fowl and vegetables to a warmed serving dish. Place the casserole on the hob (stovetop) and boil the juices over a high heat until they are reduced by about half.

8 Stir in the peas and cook gently for 2–3 minutes, then stir in the mustard. Taste and adjust the seasoning if necessary. Stir in most of the parsley and all of the mint. Pour this sauce over the guinea fowl or return the portions and vegetables to the casserole. Sprinkle over the remaining parsley and serve immediately.

VARIATIONS
• Substitute chicken or rabbit portions for the guinea fowl.
• If pancetta is unavailable, use bacon.

INGREDIENTS | **SERVES FOUR**

45ml/3 tbsp olive oil

115g/4oz pancetta, cut into lardons

30ml/2 tbsp plain (all-purpose) flour

1.2–1.6kg/2½–3½lb guinea fowl, each cut in 4 portions

1 onion, chopped

1 garlic bulb, separated into cloves and peeled

1 bottle (750ml/1¼ pints/ 3 cups) dry white wine

fresh thyme sprig

1 fresh bay leaf

a few fresh parsley sprigs

250g/9oz baby carrots

250g/9oz baby turnips

6 slender leeks, cut into 7.5cm/3in lengths

250g/9oz/2¼ cups shelled peas

15ml/1 tbsp French herb mustard

15g/½oz/½ cup fresh flat leaf parsley, chopped

15ml/1 tbsp chopped fresh mint

salt and ground black pepper

Mediterranean Duck with Harissa and Saffron

Harissa is a fiery chilli sauce from North Africa and the Middle East. Mixed with cinnamon, saffron and preserved lemon, it gives this colourful casserole an unforgettable flavour.

1 Heat the olive oil in a large, flameproof casserole. Add the duck quarters and cook on a medium heat until evenly browned all over. Remove the duck with tongs or a slotted spoon and set aside on kitchen paper to drain.

2 Add the onion slices and garlic to the oil remaining in the casserole and cook over a low heat, stirring occasionally, for about 5 minutes, until softened but not browned. Add the ground cumin and cook, stirring constantly, for 2 minutes.

3 Pour in the duck or chicken stock and stir in the lemon juice, then add the harissa, cinnamon and saffron and stir well to mix. Bring to the boil.

4 Return the duck quarters to the casserole and add the black and green olives, preserved lemon rind and lemon slices. Season to taste with salt and pepper and stir again to mix well.

5 Lower the heat, partially cover the casserole and simmer gently for about 45 minutes, or until the duck is cooked through. Discard the cinnamon stick. Stir in the chopped coriander and garnish with the coriander leaves.

COOK'S TIPS

• The term "duck" refers to birds over two months old. The rich flavour of duck is best appreciated when a duck reaches its full-grown size. Look for a duck with a supple, waxy skin with a dry appearance. It should have a long body with meaty breasts.

• A Moroccan speciality, preserved lemons are available from delicatessens and many supermarkets. They are packed in salt and will keep for up to a year. To use them, remove as many as you require from the jar and rinse well under cold running water. Remove and discard the pulp, then chop or slice the rind as required.

• For an authentic flavour, try to find light brown Moroccan olives rather than black.

INGREDIENTS | SERVES FOUR

15ml/1 tbsp olive oil

1.8–2kg/4–4^{1}/$_{2}$lb duck, quartered

1 large onion, thinly sliced

1 garlic clove, crushed

2.5ml/^{1}/$_{2}$ tsp ground cumin

400ml/14fl oz/1^{2}/$_{3}$ cups duck or chicken stock

juice of ^{1}/$_{2}$ lemon

5–10ml/1–2 tsp harissa (chilli sauce)

1 cinnamon stick

5ml/1 tsp saffron threads

50g/2oz/^{1}/$_{2}$ cup black olives

50g/2oz/^{1}/$_{2}$ cup green olives

rind of 1 preserved lemon, rinsed, drained and cut into fine strips

2–3 lemon slices

30ml/2 tbsp chopped fresh coriander (cilantro), plus extra leaves to garnish

salt and ground black pepper

Marinated Pigeon in Red Wine

The time taken to marinate and cook this casserole is well rewarded by the fabulous rich flavour of the finished dish. Stir-fried green cabbage and celeriac purée make delicious accompaniments.

INGREDIENTS | **SERVES FOUR**

4 pigeons (squab), about 225g/8oz each

30ml/2 tbsp olive oil

1 onion, coarsely chopped

225g/8oz/3¼ cups chestnut mushrooms, sliced

15ml/1 tbsp plain (all-purpose) flour

300ml/½ pint/1¼ cups game stock

30ml/2 tbsp chopped fresh parsley

salt and ground black pepper

fresh flat leaf parsley, to garnish

FOR THE MARINADE

15ml/1 tbsp light olive oil

1 onion, chopped

1 carrot, chopped

1 celery stick, chopped

3 garlic cloves, sliced

6 allspice berries, lightly crushed

2 bay leaves

8 black peppercorns, lightly crushed

150ml/¼ pint/⅔ cup red wine vinegar

150ml/¼ pint/⅔ cup red wine

45ml/3 tbsp redcurrant jelly

1 First, make the marinade. Mix together all the marinade ingredients in a large, non-metallic bowl, whisking lightly to combine.

2 Add the pigeons and turn them in the marinade to coat, then cover the bowl with clear film (plastic wrap) and set aside in the refrigerator for about 12 hours, turning the pigeons frequently so that they are well coated in the marinade.

3 Preheat the oven to 150°C/300°F/Gas 2. Heat the olive oil in a large, flameproof casserole, add the onion and mushrooms and cook over a low heat, stirring occasionally, for about 5 minutes, or until the onion has softened but not browned.

4 Meanwhile, drain the pigeons reserving the marinade. Pat the pigeons dry with kitchen paper and set aside. Then, strain the marinade into a jug (pitcher) or clean bowl and set aside. Discard the vegetables and spices in the strainer.

5 Sprinkle the flour over the pigeons and add them to the casserole, breast sides down. Pour in the marinade and stock and add the chopped parsley. Season to taste with salt and pepper. Cover and cook in the oven for 2½ hours.

6 Remove the casserole from the oven and taste and adjust the seasoning if necessary. Then serve the pigeons on warmed plates with the sauce spooned over them. Garnish with flat leaf parsley.

VARIATIONS

• If you are unable to buy pigeon, this recipe works equally well with chicken or rabbit. Buy portions and make deep slashes in the flesh so that the marinade soaks into and flavours the centre of the pieces of meat.

• For a slightly different, but no less delicious, flavour substitute juniper berries for the allspice, balsamic vinegar for the red wine vinegar and ruby port for the red wine, all of which complement pigeon well.

FISH and SHELLFISH

These recipes feature traditional cooking methods, flavours and ingredients from around the world. Goan Fish Casserole or Seafood Tagine make sophisticated and impressive dishes. The short preparation and cooking times make them suitable for occasions when time is precious, such as after work or when entertaining friends and family.

Moroccan Fish Tagine

This spicy, aromatic dish proves just how exciting an ingredient fish can be. Serve the tagine with couscous flavoured with chopped fresh mint for an authentic North African main course.

1 First make the harissa (chilli sauce). Put all the ingredients in a food processor or blender and process to a smooth paste.

2 Remove any remaining pinbones from the fish and cut it into 5cm/2in chunks. Put the chunks of fish in a wide bowl and add 30ml/2 tbsp of the harissa. Toss well to coat, cover with clear film (plastic wrap) and set aside in the refrigerator for at least 1 hour, or overnight if possible.

3 Heat half the oil in a heavy pan or flameproof casserole. Add the onions and cook over a low heat, stirring occasionally, for about 10 minutes, until golden brown. Stir in the remaining harissa and cook, stirring occasionally, for a further 5 minutes.

4 Heat the remaining olive oil in a shallow frying pan. Add the aubergine cubes and cook for about 10 minutes, until they are golden brown. Add the cubed courgettes and cook for a further 2 minutes.

5 Tip the mixture into the pan or casserole and combine with the onions, then stir in the chopped tomatoes, passata and fish stock. Bring to the boil, then lower the heat and simmer for about 20 minutes, until the flavours have developed.

6 Stir the fish chunks and preserved lemon into the pan. Add the olives and stir gently. Cover and simmer over a low heat for about 15–20 minutes, until the fish is just cooked through. Season to taste with salt and pepper. Stir in the chopped coriander. Serve with couscous, if you like, and garnish with fresh coriander sprigs.

COOK'S TIPS

• To make the fish go further, add 225g/8oz/ 1¼ cups cooked chickpeas to the tagine.
• To cook the couscous, rinse it well under cold running water, then place in a strainer or steamer lined with muslin (cheesecloth) and steam it over the tagine for about 8–10 minutes, until tender and fluffed up.

INGREDIENTS | SERVES EIGHT

1.3kg/3lb firm white fish fillets, skinned

60ml/4 tbsp olive oil

4 onions, chopped

1 large aubergine (eggplant), cut into 1cm/½in cubes

2 courgettes (zucchini), cut into 1cm/½in cubes

400g/14oz can chopped tomatoes

400ml/14fl oz/1²/₃ cups passata (bottled strained tomatoes)

200ml/7fl oz/scant 1 cup fish stock

1 preserved lemon, chopped

90g/3½oz/½ cup olives

60ml/4 tbsp chopped fresh coriander (cilantro)

salt and ground black pepper

fresh coriander sprigs, to garnish

FOR THE HARISSA

3 large fresh red chillies, seeded and chopped

3 garlic cloves, peeled

15ml/1 tbsp ground coriander

30ml/2 tbsp ground cumin

5ml/1 tsp ground cinnamon

grated rind of 1 lemon

30ml/2 tbsp sunflower oil

Goan Fish Casserole

Goa, a region in the south of India, was formerly a Portuguese colony and the cooking of the region is still a mixture of Portuguese and Indian; the addition of tamarind gives a slightly sour note to this spicy coconut sauce.

1 Mix together the turmeric and salt in a bowl. Place the fish in a shallow dish and sprinkle over the lemon juice and rub in the turmeric and salt mixture. Cover the dish and chill until needed.

2 Put the cumin, coriander and peppercorns in a blender or food processor and process to a powder. Add the garlic and ginger and process for a few seconds more.

3 Preheat the oven to 200°C/400°F/Gas 6. Mix the tamarind paste with the hot water and set aside.

4 Heat the oil in a frying pan, add the onions and cook for 5–6 minutes, until softened and golden. Transfer the onions to a shallow earthenware dish.

5 Add the fish to the oil remaining in the pan and cook briefly over a high heat, turning to seal on all sides. Remove the fish from the pan and place on top of the onions.

6 Add the ground spice mixture to the frying pan and cook over a medium heat, stirring constantly, for 1–2 minutes. Add the tamarind liquid, coconut milk and chilli strips and bring to the boil. Pour the sauce over the fish.

7 Cover the earthenware dish and cook the fish casserole in the oven for about 10 minutes. Add the prawns, pushing them into the liquid, then cover the dish again and return it to the oven for a further 5 minutes, or until the prawns turn pink. Do not overcook them or they will toughen. Taste and adjust the seasoning if necessary, sprinkle with coriander leaves and serve.

COOK'S TIP

• Tamarind has a sour yet fruity taste and is often used in curries and spicy dishes.

VARIATION

• Any firm white fish, such as cod, halibut or hake, can be used instead of monkfish.

INGREDIENTS | SERVES FOUR

7.5ml/1½ tsp ground turmeric

5ml/1 tsp salt

450g/1lb monkfish fillet, cut into 8 pieces

15ml/1 tbsp lemon juice

5ml/1 tsp cumin seeds

5ml/1 tsp coriander seeds

5ml/1 tsp black peppercorns

1 garlic clove, chopped

5cm/2in piece of fresh root ginger, finely chopped

25g/1oz tamarind paste

150ml/¼ pint/⅔ cup hot water

30ml/2 tbsp vegetable oil

2 onions, halved and sliced lengthways

400ml/14fl oz/1⅔ cups coconut milk

4 mild green chillies, seeded and cut into thin strips

16 large raw prawns (shrimp), peeled

30ml/2 tbsp chopped fresh coriander (cilantro) leaves, to garnish

Seafood Tagine

The distinctive mixture of spices and chillies used in this tagine is known as charmoula – a classic Moroccan marinade for fish, meat and vegetables. It is an especially popular way of flavouring fish and shellfish.

INGREDIENTS | **SERVES FOUR**

60ml/4 tbsp olive oil

4 garlic cloves, sliced

1–2 green chillies, seeded and chopped

a large handful of flat leaf parsley, coarsely chopped

5ml/1 tsp coriander seeds

2.5ml/^{1}/$_2$ tsp ground allspice

6 cardamom pods, split open

2.5ml/^{1}/$_2$ tsp ground turmeric

15ml/1 tbsp lemon juice

350g/12oz scorpion fish (see variations), cut into large chunks

225g/8oz squid, cleaned and cut into rings

1 onion, chopped

4 tomatoes, seeded and chopped

300ml/^{1}/$_2$ pint/1^1/$_4$ cups warm fish or vegetable stock

225g/8oz large, raw prawns (shrimp)

15ml/1 tbsp chopped fresh coriander (cilantro)

salt and ground black pepper

lemon wedges, to garnish

couscous or rice and crusty bread, to serve

1 Place the olive oil, garlic, chillies, parsley, coriander seeds, allspice and cardamom pods in a mortar and pound to a smooth paste using a pestle. Stir in the ground turmeric, salt, pepper and lemon juice.

2 Place the fish and squid in a non-metallic bowl, add the spice paste and stir. Cover and marinate in the refrigerator for 2 hours.

3 Place the onion, tomatoes and stock in a tagine or ovenproof dish and cover. Place in an unheated oven and set the oven to 200°C/400°F/Gas 6. Cook for 20 minutes.

4 Drain the fish and set aside the squid and marinade. Place the fish in the dish with the vegetables. Cover and bake for 5 minutes.

5 Add the prawns, squid rings and the remaining marinade to the dish and stir to combine. Cover the tagine and return it to the oven for 5–10 minutes, or until the fish, prawns and squid are cooked through.

6 Taste the sauce and season if necessary, then stir in the chopped coriander. Serve immediately, garnished with lemon wedges.

COOK'S TIPS

• A tagine is a shallow earthenware cooking dish with a tall, conical, earthenware lid in which the stew is traditionally cooked. A shallow ovenproof dish or a soaked, shallow clay pot can be used in its place.

• To bone the fish, lay the fillets on a board, skin side down, and run your hand gently over the flesh. Remove any bones with your fingertips or tweezers.

VARIATION

• Scorpion fish is often difficult to obtain outside the Mediterranean region. Scorpion fish is also known as racasse and is something of an acquired taste. However, this tagine is also very good made with other fish, such as red mullet, snapper, red bream, porgy or even halved cod or hake steaks.

Octopus Stew

This rustic Mediterranean casserole is a perfect dish for entertaining as it tastes even better when it has been made a day in advance. Serve with a colourful salad of baby chard, rocket and radicchio.

1 Cut the octopus into large pieces, put these in a pan and pour in sufficient cold water to cover. Season with salt, bring to the boil, then lower the heat and simmer gently for about 30 minutes to tenderize. Drain and cut into bitesize pieces.

2 Heat the olive oil in a large shallow pan. Add the red onion and cook, stirring occasionally, for 2–3 minutes, until lightly coloured, then add the garlic and cook for 1 minute more. Add the pieces of octopus and cook for 2–3 minutes, stirring and tossing constantly to colour it lightly and evenly on all sides.

3 Pour the brandy over the octopus and ignite it. When the flames have died down, add the wine, bring to the boil and bubble gently for about 5 minutes.

4 Stir in the tomatoes, with the chilli, if using, then add the potatoes, rosemary and thyme. Simmer for 5 minutes.

5 Pour in the fish stock and season with salt and pepper. Cover the pan and simmer for 20–30 minutes, stirring occasionally. The octopus and potatoes should be very tender and the sauce should have thickened slightly. At this stage, you can leave the stew to cool, then put it in the refrigerator overnight.

6 Preheat a grill (broiler) to medium-hot. To make the garlic croûtes, cut the garlic clove in half and rub both sides of the slices of baguette or ciabatta with the cut sides. Crush the garlic, stir it into the oil and brush the mixture over both sides of the bread. Grill (broil) on both sides until the croûtes are golden brown and crisp.

7 To serve the stew reheat it gently if it has been in the refrigerator overnight, taste and adjust the seasoning if necessary and stir in the parsley leaves. Serve piping hot in individual warmed bowls, garnished with rosemary sprigs and accompanied by the warm garlic croûtes.

INGREDIENTS | **SERVES FOUR**

1kg/2¼lb octopus, cleaned

45ml/3 tbsp olive oil

1 large red onion, chopped

3 garlic cloves, finely chopped

30ml/2 tbsp brandy

300ml/½ pint/1¼ cups dry white wine

800g/1¾lb ripe plum tomatoes, peeled and chopped or 2 400g/14oz cans chopped tomatoes

1 fresh red chilli, seeded and chopped (optional)

450g/1lb small new potatoes

15ml/1 tbsp chopped fresh rosemary

15ml/1 tbsp fresh thyme leaves

1.2 litres/2 pints/5 cups fish stock

30ml/2 tbsp fresh flat leaf parsley leaves

salt and ground black pepper

fresh rosemary sprigs, to garnish

FOR THE GARLIC CROÛTES

1 fat garlic clove, peeled

8 thick slices of baguette or ciabatta

30ml/2 tbsp olive oil

VEGETABLES

These versatile vegetable casseroles are the perfect dishes to
prepare when there is a vegetarian in the family or at your
dinner party. Serve the casserole as a main course with rice
or potatoes for vegetarians and as an accompaniment to
grilled meat or chicken for the meat eaters.

Vegetable Stew with Roasted Tomato and Garlic Sauce

INGREDIENTS | SERVES SIX

45ml/3 tbsp olive oil

250g/9oz shallots, peeled but left whole

1 large onion, chopped

2 garlic cloves, chopped

5ml/1 tsp cumin seeds

5ml/1 tsp ground coriander

5ml/1 tsp paprika

5cm/2in piece cinnamon stick

2 fresh bay leaves

300–450ml/$^1/_2$–$^3/_4$ pint/ 1$^1/_4$–scant 2 cups good-quality vegetable stock

good pinch of saffron threads

450g/1lb carrots, thickly sliced

2 green (bell) peppers, seeded and thickly sliced

115g/4oz/$^1/_2$ cup ready-to-eat dried apricots, halved if large

5–7.5ml/1–1$^1/_2$ tsp toasted and ground cumin seeds

450g/1lb squash, peeled, seeded and cut into chunks

pinch of sugar, to taste

25g/1oz/2 tbsp butter (optional)

salt and ground black pepper

45ml/3 tbsp fresh coriander (cilantro) leaves, to garnish

FOR THE SAUCE

1kg/2$^1/_4$lb tomatoes, halved

5ml/1 tsp sugar

45ml/3 tbsp olive oil

1–2 fresh red chillies, seeded and chopped

2-3 garlic cloves, chopped

5ml/1 tsp fresh thyme leaves

This aromatic stew makes a perfect match for couscous, enriched with a little butter or olive oil. Add some chopped fresh coriander and a handful each of raisins and toasted pine nuts to the couscous to make it special.

1 Preheat the oven to 180°C/350°F/Gas 4. First make the sauce. Place the tomatoes, cut sides uppermost, in a roasting pan. Season well with salt and pepper and sprinkle over the sugar, then drizzle with the olive oil. Roast for 30 minutes.

2 Sprinkle the chillies, garlic and thyme over the tomatoes, stir to mix and roast for a further 30–45 minutes, until the tomatoes have collapsed but are still a little juicy. Cool, then process in a food processor or blender to make a thick sauce. Sieve the sauce to remove the seeds.

3 Heat 30ml/2 tbsp of the oil in a large, wide pan or deep frying pan and cook the shallots over a medium heat, stirring occasionally, until browned all over. Remove from the pan and set aside. Add the chopped onion to the pan and cook over a low heat for 5–7 minutes, until softened. Stir in the garlic and the plain cumin seeds and cook for a further 3–4 minutes.

4 Add the coriander, paprika, cinnamon stick and bay leaves. Cook, stirring constantly, for 2 minutes more, then add the stock, saffron, carrots and green peppers. Season well, cover and simmer gently for 10 minutes.

5 Add the apricots, 5ml/1 tsp of the toasted cumin, the browned shallots and the squash. Stir in the tomato sauce. Cover and cook for a further 5 minutes. Uncover the pan and continue to simmer, stirring occasionally, for 10–15 minutes, until the vegetables are cooked.

6 Taste the stew and adjust the seasoning if necessary. Discard the cinnamon stick. Stir in the butter, if using. Serve sprinkled with coriander leaves.

VARIATION

• Try 2 medium aubergines (eggplant) and 500g/1$^1/_4$lb potatoes instead of the carrots and apricots. Cook the aubergine with the shallots and add the potatoes with the squash.

Thai Sweet Potato Stew with Garlic and Coconut Milk

Inspired by Thai cooking, this aubergine and sweet potato casserole cooked in a coconut sauce is scented with fragrant lemon grass, ginger and garlic. It is blissfully easy to prepare, yet tastes simply wonderful.

1 Heat half the oil in a wide pan or deep, lidded frying pan. Add the aubergines and cook over a medium heat, stirring occasionally, for about 5 minutes, until lightly browned on all sides. Remove from the pan and set aside.

2 Slice 4–5 of the shallots and set aside. Cook the whole shallots in the oil remaining in the pan, adding a little more oil if necessary, stirring occasionally until lightly browned. Set aside with the aubergines. Add the remaining oil to the pan and cook the sliced shallots, fennel seeds, garlic and ginger over a low heat, stirring occasionally, until soft but not browned.

3 Add the vegetable stock, lemon grass, chopped coriander stalks and any roots, the lime leaves and the whole chillies. Stir thoroughly, then cover and simmer over a low heat for 5 minutes.

4 Stir in 30ml/2 tbsp of the curry paste and then add the sweet potatoes. Simmer gently for about 10 minutes, then return the aubergines to the pan together with the browned whole shallots and cook for a further 5 minutes.

5 Stir in the coconut milk and the sugar. Season to taste, then stir in the mushrooms and simmer for 5 minutes, or until all the vegetables are cooked.

6 Stir in more curry paste and lime juice to taste, followed by the chopped coriander leaves. Taste and adjust the seasoning if necessary and ladle the vegetables into warmed bowls. Sprinkle basil leaves over the vegetables and serve immediately.

COOK'S TIP
• Thai green curry paste, based on green chillies, is available from supermarkets.

INGREDIENTS | SERVES SIX

60ml/4 tbsp vegetable oil

400g/14oz baby aubergines (eggplant), halved

225g/8oz red shallots

5ml/1 tsp fennel seeds, crushed

4–5 garlic cloves, thinly sliced

25ml/1 1/2 tbsp finely chopped fresh root ginger

475ml/15fl oz/2 cups vegetable stock

2 lemon grass stalks, outer layers discarded, chopped

15g/1/2oz/1/2 cup fresh coriander (cilantro), stalks and leaves chopped separately

3 kaffir lime leaves, bruised

2–3 small whole red chillies

45–60ml/3–4 tbsp Thai green curry paste

675g/1 1/2lb sweet potatoes, peeled and cut into chunks

400ml/14fl oz/1 2/3 cups coconut milk

2.5–5ml/1/2–1 tsp sugar

250g/9oz/4 cups thickly sliced mushrooms

juice of 1 lime, to taste

salt and ground black pepper

18 fresh Thai basil leaves or ordinary basil, to serve

Harvest Vegetable and Lentil Casserole

This easy-to-prepare meal is delicious served with warm garlic bread. If you really want to make the most of the tomato flavour, add a few sun-dried tomatoes with the lentils.

1 Preheat the oven to 180°C/350°F/Gas 4. Heat the sunflower or olive oil in a large, flameproof casserole. Add the leeks, garlic and celery, and cook over a low heat, stirring occasionally with a wooden spoon, for about 3 minutes, until the leeks are just beginning to soften.

2 Add the carrots, parsnips, sweet potato, swede, brown or green lentils, tomatoes, thyme, marjoram and vegetable stock and season to taste with salt and pepper. Stir the vegetables well to combine. Bring to the boil over a medium heat, stirring occasionally with a wooden spoon to make sure that the vegetables do not stick to the base of the casserole.

3 Cover and bake for about 50 minutes, until the vegetables and lentils are cooked through and tender, removing the casserole from the oven and gently stirring the vegetable mixture once or twice during the cooking time.

4 Remove the casserole from the oven. Mix the cornflour with 45ml/3 tbsp cold water in a small bowl to make a smooth paste. Stir the mixture into the casserole and heat on the hob (stovetop), stirring until the mixture comes to the boil and thickens, then simmer gently for 2 minutes, stirring constantly. Taste and adjust the seasoning if necessary, then serve in warmed bowls. Hand around garlic bread.

COOK'S TIPS
• Green and brown lentils, unlike red lentils, keep their shape during cooking and are good for soups, salads and casseroles. Green lentils have a delicate flavour, while brown ones have a rather more earthy taste.
• To make garlic bread, beat 115g/4oz/½ cup softened butter until creamy, then beat in 2 crushed garlic cloves and 30ml/2 tbsp chopped fresh parsley. Slice a baguette almost all the way through, coat the slices with garlic butter, wrap in foil and bake at 180°C/350°F/Gas 4 for 10–15 minutes.

INGREDIENTS | SERVES SIX

15ml/1 tbsp sunflower or olive oil

2 leeks, sliced

1 garlic clove, crushed

4 celery sticks, chopped

2 carrots, sliced

2 parsnips, diced

1 sweet potato, diced

225g/8oz swede (rutabaga), diced

175g/6oz/³/₄ cup whole brown or green lentils

450g/1lb tomatoes, peeled, seeded and chopped

15ml/1 tbsp chopped fresh thyme

15ml/1 tbsp chopped fresh marjoram

900ml/1½ pints/3¾ cups vegetable stock

15ml/1 tbsp cornflour (cornstarch)

45ml/3 tbsp water

salt and ground black pepper

warm garlic bread, to serve

Jamaican Black Bean Pot

Molasses imparts a rich treacly flavour to the spicy sauce, which incorporates a stunning mix of black beans, vibrant red and yellow peppers and orange butternut squash.

INGREDIENTS | **SERVES FOUR**

225g/8oz/1¼ cups dried black beans

1 bay leaf

30ml/2 tbsp vegetable oil

1 large onion, chopped

1 garlic clove, chopped

5ml/1 tsp mustard powder

15ml/1 tbsp molasses or black treacle

30ml/2 tbsp soft dark brown sugar

5ml/1 tsp dried thyme

2.5ml/½ tsp dried chilli flakes

5ml/1 tsp vegetable stock (bouillon) powder

1 red (bell) pepper, seeded and diced

1 yellow (bell) pepper, seeded and diced

675g/1½lb butternut squash or pumpkin, seeded and cut into 1cm/½in dice

salt and ground black pepper

fresh thyme sprigs, to garnish

plain boiled rice or cornbread, to serve

1 Soak the beans overnight in plenty of water, then drain and rinse well under cold running water. Place them in a large pan, pour in fresh cold water to cover and add the bay leaf. Bring to the boil, then boil rapidly for 10 minutes. Reduce the heat, cover the pan, and simmer for about 30 minutes until tender. Drain, reserving the cooking water. Preheat the oven to 180°C/350°F/Gas 4.

2 Heat the vegetable oil in a flameproof casserole, add the onion and garlic and cook over a low heat, stirring occasionally, for about 5 minutes, until softened. Stir in the mustard powder, molasses or treacle, sugar, dried thyme, chilli flakes and seasoning. Cook for about 1 minute, stirring, then mix in the black beans.

3 Add enough water to the reserved liquid to make 400ml/14fl oz/1⅔ cups, mix in the stock powder and pour into the casserole. Bake in the oven for 25 minutes.

4 Add the peppers and the squash or pumpkin and mix well. Cover, then bake for a further 45 minutes.

5 Taste and adjust the seasoning if necessary and make sure the squash is tender. Garnish with thyme and serve with rice or cornbread.

COOK'S TIPS

• To prepare squash or pumpkin, cut it in half using a large sharp knife, then peel off the skin. Remove the seeds using a spoon and slice the flesh into chunks. Choose firm specimens that are blemish-free.

• If you don't have stock (bouillon) powder, then dissolve half a stock cube in the bean cooking water.

• The reason for pre-cooking the beans by boiling vigorously for 10 minutes is to destroy a naturally occurring toxin. This treatment is required for several other types of dried beans such as black and red kidney beans and borlotti beans.

Index